G000122957

THE RIVER THAMES IN VERSE

an illustrated anthology of new poems

from the River Thames Society's Open Poetry Competition
in the winter of 2002–03

EDITED BY VAL MASON

Published by the River Thames Society
with the kind sponsorship of the Thames Heritage Trust

First published in 2004 by River Thames Society
Side House, Middle Assendon, Henley-on-Thames
Oxfordshire, RG9 6AP

Digitally printed in Great Britain by Butler and Tanner,
Burgess Hill, West Sussex.

ISBN 0-9548078-0-4

Anthology © Val Mason · 2004
Foreword © Sir Anthony Durant · 2004
Design © David Woodward, Design for Print · 2004

© Copyright of the poems remains with the authors. Similarly
copyright of the illustrations remains with the artists. Prior
written permission is required for any use. Please write initially
to: River Thames Society, Side House, Middle Assendon,
Henley-on-Thames, Oxfordshire, RG9 6AP,
or email: admin@riverthamessociety.org.uk

No part of this publication may be reproduced, stored in a retrieval system, or trans-
mitted in any form or by any means, electronic, mechanical, photocopying, recording
or otherwise, without the prior written permission of the copyright owners.

This book is sold subject to the condition that it shall not by way of trade or
otherwise, be lent, resold, hired out or otherwise circulated without the
publisher's prior consent in any form of binding or cover other than that in which it
is published and without a similar condition including this condition being imposed
on the subsequent purchaser.

Acknowledgements

The River Thames Society thanks the poets and artists who have
contributed to this book and given their permission to publish
the poems and illustrations. We also thank Design for Print
for their work on the book design, David Bann for his production
advice, and Alix Horne for her administrative help. We are also
grateful to the River & Rowing Museum for their encouragement
and to Paul Coleman for the Thames Heritage Trust's support.

Thanks also go to those who helped with the Society's poetry
competition, particularly Dieter Jebens, for promoting the
competition in the Society's magazine *Thames Guardian*, and
our three judges: the preliminary judges, Jane Draycott and
Virginia Winfield, and the final judge, Wendy Cope.

For further copies

An order form is at www.riverthamessociety.org.uk or please
write for an order form to: River Thames Society, Side House,
Middle Assendon, Henley-on-Thames, Oxfordshire, RG9 6AP
or email admin@riverthamessociety.org.uk

The River Thames Society is registered as Charity No. 288380.

Foreword

The River Thames Society has since its formation created a number of initiatives: for example, the magazine, *Thames Guardian*, the Society's River Wardens on the non-tidal part of the river, and its Planning Officers along the length of the river. Recently it has added to the list the newly-created River Thames Alliance. This was co-founded by the Society, following its report commissioned from the Oxford Brookes University. We are now supporting the proposal to create a National Park in the estuary area as part of the development of the Thames Gateway.

The Society has always looked for ideas that will appeal to a wider audience among people who care for the river. Val Mason, a leading member of the Middle Thames Branch and a new Director of the Society, proposed a poetry competition. The Society supported the proposal, though we had no idea that we would receive so many excellent entries – 140 poems were submitted.

We owe a great debt to Val Mason who vigorously promoted the competition and saw it through. Val has also, with the sponsor-ship of the Thames Heritage Trust, created and published this anthology of the poems. The book is also beautifully illustrated.

I add my congratulations to the winner of the competition, Barbara Daniels, for her poem, *Homage*. It reminded me so much of the funeral of the great man, Sir Winston Churchill. I watched, in 1965, his funeral procession in Westminster Square as it passed on its way to St Paul's, and later saw from the embankment, the lowering of the dockyard cranes as the funeral barge passed on the river.

We hope that the anthology will be enjoyed by all, by those who love poetry and those who know and love the Thames. We also trust that those who read its pages will be given new inspiration to write more poems about the Thames, Britain's greatest river.

SIR ANTHONY DURANT
President of the River Thames Society
June 2004

The River Thames in Verse

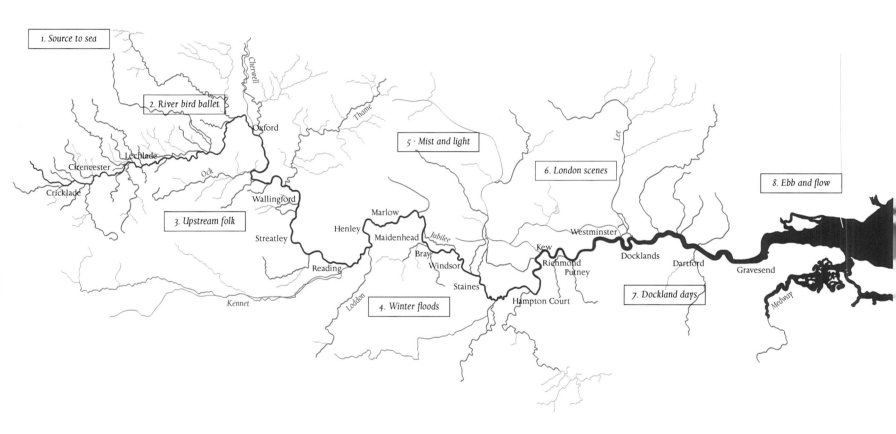

1. Source to sea

2. River bird ballet

Cherwell

Oxford

Thame

5 · Mist and light

Lee

6. London scenes

8. Ebb and flow

Lechlade

Cirencester

Ock

Cricklade

Wallingford

3. Upstream folk

Marlow

Henley

Streatley

Maidenhead

Jubilee

Westminster

Reading

Bray

Windsor

Kew

Docklands

Dartford

Richmond

Gravesend

Kennet

Loddon

Staines

Putney

4. Winter floods

Hampton Court

7. Dockland days

Medway

Contents

*NATIONAL COMPETITION PRIZE-WINNER

List of illustrations

† illustration commissioned for this anthology
§ illustration by the poet

Introduction

The River Thames in Verse is a wonderful collection of new poems inspired by the River Thames.

The collection reflects the special role that the Thames has in the nation's history and cultural heritage. It also reflects the love and respect that people have for the Thames and the important part that the river plays in their lives.

The poems are selected from the entries to a national poetry competition held in the winter of 2002–03. They include the six prize-winning poems selected by Wendy Cope, the final judge for the competition.

The selection makes fascinating reading, describing so many different aspects of the Thames. The poems are arranged in eight sections, which follow the river downstream.

Some of the poems are about the river itself on its journey of over 200 miles, from Gloucestershire through rural England, into London and then to Docklands and the estuary. Many of the poets refer to specific places, landmarks and bridges on the Thames, while others write about well-known events and popular activities along the river.

A number of the poems describe personal relationships and memories related to the river. Some are great fun, like the poem about people at the Henley Regatta. While the winning poem, *Homage*, is more reflective – it describes the river today and remembers the day of Sir Winston Churchill's funeral procession on the Thames in London.

There are also poems about the different river birds and wildlife. The many moods of the river are captured, from its peaceful, tranquil moments, to the more menacing times of the 2003 floods.

A number of the poets refer to the inspiration that the river gives to artists, and this inspiration is so clearly demonstrated by the range of illustrations in the anthology.

Just as the poems are the work of over thirty different poets, the illustrations are by a variety of artists, most of whom live and work in the Thames Valley.

Some of the illustrations have been commissioned specifically for the anthology and are inspired by particular poems. Indeed three of the poems are illustrated by the poets themselves. Others have been offered as illustrations by well-established artists. Just two illustrations were chosen from works held in museums – a Claude Monet painting of Charing Cross Bridge, and Wilfred Morden's painting of Sir Winston Churchill's funeral procession.

I do hope that readers enjoy the anthology as much as I have enjoyed compiling it, and that it will introduce them to new aspects of the Thames, and add to the nation's favourite poems.

VAL MASON
River Thames Society
June, 2004

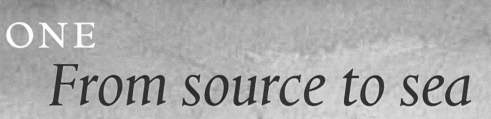

ONE
From source to sea

Liquid History

'The Thames is liquid history'
JOHN BURNS (1858–1943)

My first's in Marlow, but not Maidenhead,
throughout the South East, this landmark is spread.
My second's in Goldie, and Isis twice,
not in Boat Race, as the oars dip and slice.
My third is in voles, and in riverbed,
but not graceful swans, which beg to be fed.
My fourth's in the Dome, the Tate and the Eye,
look down on me from the wheel in the sky.
My fifth is in the bridges, Waterloo
Hungerford, Southwark, Albert, Tower too.

My next is in Dartford, and Battersea,
in Teddington, Twickenham and Streatley.
My seventh you'll go to Henley to find,
Shiplake and Cookham come not far behind.
My eighth is in water, in banks and boats
and in the Embankment, where a pub floats.
My ninth is in Richmond, but not in Kew
though the garden's glorious all year through.
My tenth is in Middlesex, and in Kent
Berkshire and Essex before I am spent.
My last is in Chertsey, Windsor and Staines,
and in my estuary, where it all drains.

My whole is somewhere I'm sure you must know,
sights on the banks of my swift Eastward flow –
Hampton Court, Eton, that view of Big Ben;
all stunning places, all put there by men.
And in the fields, the woods and the hills
winter's iced verges, and spring daffodils.
In the sailors who enjoy the summer's sun,
in cyclists and runners, all having fun.
In autumn I carry leaves on my way,
though their splendour makes me wish I could stay.
I meet with the Cherwell, Loddon and more,
into my flow, all their waters they pour.
But the way that most remember my looks,
Is 'EastEnders' ending, on tenterhooks.

GILL SMITH

Source of the Thames · DIANNE COCKBURN

Tamasá Reaches

Near the railway bridge on the road to Cirencester
you pass a sign which says, 'Source of the River Thames'.
Its underground spring comes up for breath
through banks that are hardly higher than the water.
Trout are here, otters and water voles.
Take the meandering river's path through Lechlade,
whose stone-built houses keep their hidden views,
until, near Oxford, wider waters offer
residence to house-boats, fishermen and geese.

> From Putney to Mortlake
> leaning and pulling
> oars on the rowlocks
> dipping and twisting
> past Barn Elms and Hammersmith
> sweatshirts sodden
> with splashes and straining
> megaphones shouting
> to dark blue and light blue
> victors triumphant
> stride through the water
> but slumping defeated
> the losers stay listless

Where fretful salt meets yellow-brownish sludge
The old Thames sang of rotting wood and skulls,
barbyl, flounders, spearheads, bits of rope.
Its pre-Celt name was *Tamasá*, dark river.
At this forum of city stone and water
the old trades are gone. Docks and wharves,
where two thousand masts once glittered on the water
with cargoes of tea and sugar, silk and oranges,
and steamers to the Empire bruised the oceans
with holds of steel and missionary trunks –
all are transformed by the new commerce,
the new river gods, Finance and the Media.
Below their elegant glass powerhouses
sailboards catch the wind
and wine and coffee bars displace
oyster and apple stalls
But dark *Tamasá* still has its secrets.

JENYTH WORSLEY · *Commended Prize*

Charting the Thames

Springing from nowhere
gurgling dreams of greatness,
land-locked Thame and Isis merge
their names and waters in the fledgling Thames,
        flowing towards the sea.

A Celtic signature sprawled lavishly
across the page of southern English counties
where once a different language ran;
Brythonic past and modern Essex man
        wink and join hands through history.

Swans and bottles bobbing,
willow stroking slack tide dreamily,
fish and filth weave patterns with the currents,
fresh springs and sewage race, refresh, pollute,
        flush out into the sea.

An ink-black cormorant carves an eastward flight path.
relentless arrow etched across pale sky.
What instinct guides it over fields and woodland?
How does it know which way it has to fly
        to find salt spray?

Suave spin doctors, pimps and pushers, muffled men
loitering on sleazy staircases, still slip
their guilt and plots beneath the oily surface of a working river,
which smiles benignly, won't divulge their secrets
        as it flows towards the sea.

Sky-scrapers and warehouses draw the line
tracing an artery of a nation's beating heart.
It hooks an Eye then bows beneath a Dome,
artlessly scribbling curves and loops, to leap
        the Barrier in its way.

A tanker, shadowed by a sailing boat,
melts in the mist that masks receding land.
Strong tides now pull and tease identity,
mixing salt and brackish water in the estuary
        and seasoning the sea.

ALWYN MARRIAGE

The Thames Rivers

Some fifty rivers help the Thames to swell towards the sea.
From the source, towards the locks, they start off with the Key
In turn, the Churn, Ray, Cole and Coln (the one without an 'e')
Leach, Windrush and Evenlode, how good's your memory?

I'm only listing rivers, not the brooks or creeks or streams,
Nor canals or drains or other engineering schemes,
Nor side headwater rivers, just those with confluent seams
(even when interment has been taken to extremes).

No Oxford brooks for Oxford dons: here Cherwell joins the game
Downstream find the Ock and Thame – how singular the name –
After a Pang (but not a Bourne) the Kennet joins the frame
And Loddon feeds black water both day and night the same.

Next Wick and Wye and Wraysbury, think treble W
'What of Jubilee?' you cry, should that thought trouble you
'Tis just a bypass channel that floods can bubble through
(Woe betide the downstream home henceforth a puddle too)

The Shire River boundary (now 'County Ditch') at Staines
River Colne (with 'e') fields north-west London's rains
The Chertsey Abbey and forked Bourne ensure confusion reigns
Likewise 'Wey, the Engine, Ash' has nowt to do with trains.

Together Mole and Ember, not truly on their own,
Rythe, Hogsmill and Longford in the last non-tidal zone.
Upon the ebb, at Isleworth, a Crane is not alone
Here the Dukes, then Brent and Wandle, plus malted cologne.

Seek London's buried rivers, like Graveney, Effra, Fleet,
Shoreditch, Walbrook and Neckinger somewhere beneath your feet,
The Tyburn and the Ravensbourne, I'm told that one was Sweet,
Ranelagh runs in tubes through Tubes, will not admit defeat.

Returning to the open air, the Pool and Lee are dank
Roding, Beam and Inglebourne all drain the northern flank
Whilst Cray and Darent pour from Kent, and for your time I thank:
Headway from the Medway ends this verse at Doggerel Bank.

GEOFF PAYNE

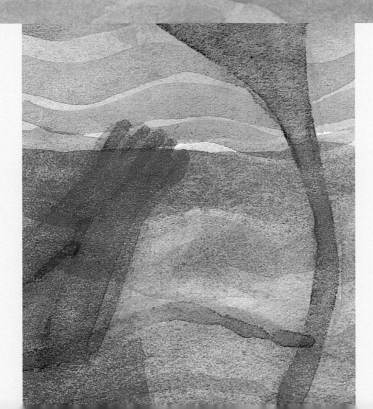

TWO
River bird ballet

Memory of Migration

Low over the water Canada geese,
three V formations,
wartime flights of fighters.
This is September
over an English river.

Yesterday they flew at speed
to the water meadows
a spare mile upstream,
only to return
to the wooded banks.

Today in sunlight, again
the perfect V's,
adaptation or memory the victor.
Why the misty dream of flight
to a hotter land?

Winter here on the Thames,
is well lardered and warm enough,
no need to move with the seasons.
Memory is ignored
but the practice flights go on.

ELIZABETH BELL

River Praise

God's grebe parts the river
and diving sings:
"Trust in the Lord,
the giver of all good things!"

"Be still," sighs the heron,
in the holy willow tree.
The cormorant lifts its wings
in worship: "Taste and see!"

Seagulls speak God's mercy
into every wind:
"Seek, seek, seek,
and you shall find!"

The kingfisher flies love's banner
in this celebration:
a flash of the heart's fire,
at Christ's coronation!

BARRIE ARMSTRONG

Kingfishers · ROGER BARNES

Two Cormorants

Two intermittent cormorants pop up
    then duck-dive down, and sometimes coincide
to gulp their catch together, silver scraps,
    before at once submerging in the tide.
Their promptitude in plunging down implies
    water may hide a more congenial place
that shields from teasing wind and freezing skies
    the flying ballet of the streamlined race.
There food is plentiful, and social life
    is possible. On days of sultry heat
the river's tent is cool, its skylit roof
    illuminates their underwater flight
through the unfailing pantry of fresh fish
beneath the cover of the river-dish.

ANNA ADAMS

Cormorants diving · ANNA ADAMS

Legless ballet · Dianne Cockburn

The Legless Ballet

Fine floss of mist dissolving, exposes sixty mute swans
Dappling the flood-meadow, alabaster on sage green,
Each individual preoccupied with personal hygiene
Rather than choreography – and yet a languid legless ballet
Has evolved, as single wings fan up like sails, are subject to
Meticulous inspection, then refurled, flush with the bodyline.
Beaks operate like multi-purpose pocket knives, now stabbing
The surrounding grass, now turning feathers over,
Delicate as a philatelist inspecting priceless acquisitions.
Then a display of neck aerobics, serpentine gyrations,
Musculature apparent, although never overemphasised.
No flight of fancy, or of fact, disturbs the tableau,
Save for a droning Hercules, camouflaged ugly duckling,
Banking towards Wiltshire, the aircrew barely registering
The placid, empty Thames, white spots on grassland.

PETER WYTON

THREE
Upstream folk

Autumn

Today we'll take the round walk
keeping the river on our left,
the stiff wind in our faces.

The summer people, shallow and ubiquitous,
are gone now.
We can reclaim our territory.

The wind in our faces,
our lips numb,
it's hard to speak of what's important.

We'll try again when we've
made the loop. The wind at our backs,
we can turn up our collars for shelter.

The dogs stay close at our heels,
studying your serious face.
They've eavesdropped on our summer.

Will you stay another year?
You've talked of a trip
around the world.

The Canada geese flap and cry,
causing the dogs to grumble.
We're watching your face for clues.

I slip on a mud patch,
lose my balance,
clutch your hand for support.

Unexpectedly, you're back,
your arm across my shoulders,
your face open again.

We'll need wood in for winter,
you say.

WENDY KLEIN

Halfpenny Bridge

Halfpenny Bridge was very new,
When it was built in ninety-two.
Seventeen ninety-two I mean.
The locals made an awful scene
When the ferry crossing to the town
Had been officially shut down.
Far too deep to ford in waders
The only route for all the traders
Was over the bridge, and through the toll
Levied at one halfpenny per soul
Horses were charged two-pence each way
So much to pay each market day.
Carriages were welcomed here
At sixpence the crossing cost them dear.
But for going to church there was no fee,
The blessed journey was quite free.

Now when Napoleon at last was beat
Poor men returned with little to eat
So this crippling toll they had to stop;
Halfpence, whenever you went to shop!
In thirty-nine they won the day
Once the old soldiers had their say.
Now modern cars may cross quite free,
Thanks to those who cancelled the fee.

GRAHAM KNIGHT

Halfpenny bridge · ROGER BARNES

Riverside Living

I am living by the riverside,
achieved my dream at last.
For many years I fancied it
and many years have passed

Some say I'm in my dotage,
some say it's just a whim.
Friend David says it's super
and I agree with him.

I can sit and watch the water
or feed the ducks with bread.
There is no fear of boredom,
that never can be said.

When I watch the water
and its continual flow,
it helps to make me realise
just how little I know.

It also makes me realise
what a tiny cog I am.
The water flows on year by year
and doesn't give a damn.

I moved in just three weeks ago
and soon it will be spring.
Then I can watch the daffodils
and hear the birds all sing.

There will be other noises
to supplement the ducks
and the seagulls' raucous squawking
when they have their daily rucks.

The chug of many pleasure boats,
the oarsfolk as they strain
and 'Dolly Birds' in bikinis
Can my binoculars take the strain?

So, I am looking forward to
this summer by the Thames.
To my fellow river lovers
as they play their summer games.

To the swans and other river birds
as they rear their broods of young
and to all the other forms of life
as the daily song is sung.

BERNARD BOYS

Under the clock · TERENCE GILBERT

Going to the Regatta

Once again the sun is scorching.
It's the first week in July.
Darling, have you seen my blazer?
Where on earth's my old school tie?

Dear old river, dear Regatta,
Thronging crowds o'er Henley Bridge.
Hats you've never seen the like of.
Champagne cooling in the 'fridge.

We'll go in the Stewards Enclosure,
What a crowd and what a din!
Look, they're measuring her hem-line.
She is out, but we are in!

Now here comes my Oxford College.
What a splendid looking crew!
Did you know that I was stroke once?
Very nearly got a 'Blue'!

Now it's time to take our luncheon
In Leander's hallowed hall.
Dear old Buffy's got our tickets.
There he is. Give him a call.

Hello Buffy! Hello Angie!
Gosh, that is a stunning dress!
Quick, Stand still! Here comes Steve Redgrave.
We may feature in the press!

Chicken, salmon, Moët et Chandon
Then a glass of vintage port.
Hardly know some of these fellows.
Do you think they're *quite* our sort?

Once again the racing's started.
How they strain to win the prize!
Yes, these deck-chairs are quite comfy.
Maybe I'll just close my eyes.

Tea already? How time's flying!
We must think of going soon.
But I'll not forget the sunshine
Of this lovely afternoon.

Time to go. Ah, here's the Volvo
Darling, would you like to drive?
What a queue! Where do they all go?
Straight down the M twenty-five!

ROBERT DE BOARD

FOUR
Winter floods

The River God

Ha Ha! I'm back you see
my power just grows you won't tame me
I stake my claim through storm and rain
to drown the valleys and flood the plains
I'm in full flow – I'll do my worst
then rise so high my banks will burst

Your puny efforts at flood defence
of booms and barriers I easily drench
and sweep away and thunder-through
bridges, buildings, people too!
Rushing faster in full spate
Hmm – nice new homes to inundate
But WAIT!
There was a time man worshiped me
my course was this land's artery
that fertilised the fields and trees
and nourished your ancient societies
whose waters helped provide a wage
and fish that swam since a past ice age

But now my stream roars angrily
from spring to river and source to sea
oozing menace at every bend
so listen well *Homo sapiens*
I float your boats – I slake your thirst
and just remember...
I WAS HERE FIRST !

Les Crowhurst

Water flow · Susan Martin

On going to see the Thames in flood

Leaving the car on higher drier ground
We pull on waders well above the thigh
And stiffly set off Thamesward down the road.
Hard work to walk when water's pulling past,
Tugging at knees and pressing boots to skin
While tiring wary steps wade slowly on.

The little road dips in
And out of flood,
Smooth water hiding all the unknown depths
Where booted feet stir through the lurking mud.

Still sheets of water cover all the fields
And half-drowned grasses bristle at the brim.
A hundred seagulls wheel upon the air
Or float on their reflections in the pool,
A frothy margin lapping at the rim.
Leafless and gaunt the oak-tree, tall and bare,
Stands to its knees in water, arms aloft.

And there ahead
is Thames – but out of bed,
Topping his banks and stretching ever wide,
Greedy to claim the floodplain for his own,
Surging and smooth and silver side to side.
A raft of bubbles swells and rushes by,
And whirlpool eddies nibble at the bank.
The satin surface clear reflects the sky.
The Loddon, laden, tips into the Thames,
Adding its muddy burden to the flow
While past the swimming branches dip and roll
Pellmell towards the weir unwilling pulled.
Dread thoughts of drowning all unbidden come
With horrid fascination of the flood.

Time to return.
Back past unthreatening fields and winter trees
With sodden footsteps squelching through the swamp.
The silver mirror ripples in the breeze.
A world of unfamiliar beauty lies
Before our feet and dazzles in our eyes,
The flat familiar landscape rearranged
By magic of the water-cover changed.

JILL FINDLAY

River Thames, January 2003

They said that it would never be
A surge at Staines and Runnymede
So opened up the Jubilee
A change of course no one agreed

A surge at Staines and Runnymede
The drawing rooms are dry in Bray
A change of course no one agreed
No one agreed but all will pay.

The drawing rooms are dry in Bray
Bands H secure behind their gates
No one agreed but all will pay
All those left to their watery fates

Bands H secure behind their gates
They contemplate their great good luck
All those left to their water fates
They do not count the mass the ruck

They contemplate their great good luck
Those EA chaps who turned the tide
They do not count the mass the ruck
Statistics can be made to hide

Those EA chaps who turned the tide
Their budgets now they must align
Statistics can be made to hide
Surcharges passing down the line

Their budgets now they must align
Insurers swell their surging fee
Surcharges passing down the line
For sure they'll stop at you and me.

ANNE JENKINS

Jubilee River

The Environmental people
Came up with an idea,
We'll build a great big river
And call it Jubilee.

No more floods in Maidenhead,
And Windsor will be free,
But Arthur Walters shook his head
And said 'You wait and see!'

The rains came down from heaven,
The Thames, it rose up high,
The villagers of Wraysbury
Could only look and sigh.

The Village Hall was flooded,
And many homes were too.
Children boated on the Green
In dinghies and canoe.

The Environmental people said,
'Computers cannot lie',
But the villagers of Wraysbury said,
'Then why aren't our homes dry?'

BARBARA ABBOTT

Stranded seat · SUE MILTON

Flood sunset · SUE MILTON

The River Thames apologises

Well, I'm normally so good
It's only now and then I flood
And I'd like you all to know
How steadily I flow
In my narrow river bed
When I'd like a change instead.
My point you're bound to see
And I'm sure that you'd agree
If only you were me.

But then there comes a day
When I plot my getaway
Lapping steadily at first
So that no one fears the worst
Then I ripple far and wide
In an all-engulfing tide.
And it's great to be a sea
As I'm sure you would agree
If only you were me.

When I've had my bit of fun
And my days of flood are done
It's back I make my watery way
And half decide no more to stray
And as I sink into my bed
I vow to settle down instead.
But I do so like a spree
As I'm sure you would agree
If only you were me.

ENID PHILIP

FIVE
Mist and light

Dusk

Cast a mantle of mist on the valley
Call the sweet nightingale to its nest
Hush the last summer breeze
As it rustles the trees
For the Thames has just gone to its rest.

The song of the lark greets the morning
And the sparkle of waves needs the light
But the dance of the stars
Between Venus and Mars
Is the show for the river tonight.

So moor up the boat to the shoreline
And stack up the hay where it's threshed
Quell the barge-pilot's horn
Till the following morn,
For the Thames has just gone to its rest.

GORDON COPE

The river bank · ELIZABETH BELL

Light

Early morning mist-light,
dim sky and shadows,
all colour drained,
each nuance a shade
of grey or black,
except a faint ghost
of green on the river bank.

Noon-time light,
pearly sky, mist gone,
colours are muted,
pale greens, mid browns,
the water a dull sludge,
clear green on the river bank.

Late afternoon sunlight,
the auburn leaves gleaming,
shadows a deep purple,
treetops yellow gold,
the heron waiting,
a still grey shape
by the bright green on the river bank.

Elizabeth Bell

Winter River
(at Hampton Court)

Wake slaps the tide-slimed quay
Pale mist engulfs a creeping skiff

Damp, icy chill seeks bone
White breath hangs in air

Muffled voices ride an easterly
Swan wings thrum overhead

Earth is dun, trees stripped
The river deep, sin dark

Lights flare: azure, vermilion, gold
Colours fit for a king

JOSEPH RYAN

Fire River · SUSAN MARTIN

Painting at Kew

With an artist's palette
he orders the morning.
Yellow ochre fixes the iris
growing deep into the quiet
pools of neglected water,
sap green holds the grassy
reflection rippling at the edge,
vermilion splashes are a girl running,
her smile fixed forever.
The sun moves higher
and the river clears to ultramarine.
Only the boats break free
from the careful brushstrokes
and obey the tide.

LORNA PATTERSON

River · Suzanne-Lizette Strand

Watching the River

The sun shines down
Lights its calming waves
And I am truly spellbound,
Watching in a watery daze.

Awash with colours
Green, blue, dark and light.
I peer into its coolness
Till there is nothing else in sight.

How would it feel to slip
Beneath the murky ripples, bidden?
Sheeted like glass, tinted with depth,
Danger like an iceberg, hidden.

To fall upon this watery bed,
And sleep forever more.
Would there be rest, and peace
Far from the living shore?

LAURA KAYNE

SIX
London scenes

Thames River Odyssey

Crossing the River, bound for Waterloo,
amid decaying streets, refurbished wharves,
I see cloaked Chaucer, Pope and Daniel Defoe,
a hosed, doubleted Shakespeare striding to *The Globe*,
words afloat where Thames water flows;
pentameters, couplets and Miltonian apostrophes.
Hard by bear pits and wenches – the flowering of literary England,
London's hot sexual intrigue and machination,
poor Marlowe's sticky, pub brawl ending,
unsubsidised, pre-tabloid, South Bank shows.

Like an arrow from an Olde English bow
my mind shoots further back to Londinium settlement,
speeds on to Norman Conquest, a foreign coronation.
I see prisoners in the Tower, young pretenders,
despotic Kings and – *plus ça change* – scheming politicians;
Henry The Eighth, Thomas More and shrewd Cromwellians,
Elizabeth The First with 'the heart of a man'
transported by Thames to address her fearful nation.
Moon tidal river pulled from source to mouth
stilled only in Avercamp scenes of ice and snow.

Plague, Gunpowder Plot, Pepys and The Great Fire,
despite a tendency to iconoclasm
how can I not see '*their finest hour*':
Luftwaffe Heinkels, searchlights and barrage balloons,
'*Good old Winnie*' smoking calamus scented cigars
crouched over maps in subterranean Cabinet room
making defiant speeches sustaining London pride
under to The Underground, those poor bombed souls who died –
the unnamed, the unnumbered, the unsung.
'Great Britons' – anonymous individuals who defeated Fascism.

Time circles slowly with the fulcrum of '*The Eye*'
finds dubious expression in construction of a Dome.
As the poets and historians now testify
slave cargoes from around the world, the shame of Imperialism,
TS Eliot on the bridge seeing how many were undone.
But there are The Beatles, The Stones and Mary Quant,
1966 – Moore, Hurst and Bobby Charlton,
raincoated Terry and Julie, Waterloo's setting suns.
East of Parliament and Big Ben, coursing to the sea,
biscuit tin images, selective memories — meander on.

JULIAN COLTON

Light and shade, London '96 · Roy Hammond

View of Waterloo Bridge, from Hungerford Bridge

Over the river in five easy leaps
the concrete hurdler, like a skimming stone,
bounces four times on water, striking roots
that grow into a bridge: a mantel-shelf
of ornaments and trophies, wedding-cakes,
cheese-graters, a dome-lidded biscuit tin,
and clockwork mice that glide along the edge.
Two hours transform these things to mystery.

Now, dim in misty dusk, the great dome seems
remote as God, while floodlights show St. Bride's
as child among vast, faintly printed tombs
that hint at life within; below ebb tide –
combed by the bridges – coiling through the City –
races from Richmond to the estuary.

ANNA ADAMS · *Commended Prize*

Charing Cross Bridge, the Thames · CLAUDE MONET

'What I like most of all in London is the fog.'
(Claude Monet)

From the sixth floor of the Savoy
He strokes the fog like restless smoke
Across the Thames. An orange sun
Brushes the haze, turns water coral.
A blue spume moistens the canvas
Sliding the hours before sunset
Into a shimmering dream. Light,
Clouds and river billow past,
Vapour rolls in the air, obscures
Our boundaries. In a hundred paintings
The artist shifts his visions
Before us. Paint feathers the surface
Like a meniscus. You could walk
On the buildings, float on the sky.
In the foreground
The luminous river courses like blood.

DAPHNE SCHILLER

I want to see a daffodil on Big Ben
(for Sara Boyes)

I want to see a daffodil on Big Ben
the Thames with fairy lights
bridges leading to the sky
the dome take off –
I want to fly.

I want to see only green again
feel grass, feel tingling.
I want to *see* a breeze, *feel* yellow
understand the gull poised on a lamp
watch with its eyes
see what it sees below.

I want to grow numb, grow cold
grow in contemplation
get lost, search out daffodils again.

DOREEN KING

Big Ben fantasy · ANNIE STEVENS

Crossing to the South Bank

The river shimmers
like the charity shop dress
I wanted but didn't buy –
sinuous, glittery, needing a wash.

When would I have worn it
in my drab life?
I imagine its silver
slither down my body.

The ferris wheel
and the pretty new bridge
sparkle, the river laughs
as the wind touches it up.

I could wear the dress
in bed, rustling smooth
as a snakeskin
under your wondering hands.

ANGELA RIGBY

London Eye · SUZANNE-LIZETTE STRAND

SEVEN
Dockland days

Belonging

Best forget the dream: a gilded day with sugared grass,
our breath fluffed round our heads; a crystal glide
from underground to scatter light before we clouded it
with Grandad's dust. The infant stream had sprawled,
hidden its birth in lakes which once were fields.
The river writes the rules.

At least the wind was with us, pushing its breath
along the flow. It floated the floury particles
but left the grit to drop like winnowed grain
from the parapet of Ha'penny Bridge.
For a second, the ashes scummed the swell
that simmered east then clotted, swirled, went down
as the river received its own.

He was a Millwall man, whose living Devlin did for,
last in a line of stevedores and lightermen
with muscles like mooring ropes, hands of seasoned teak,
who'd seen the water stained with indigo, coal and blood;
and women who'd scrubbed at shirts which smelled of lemons,
cinnamon, tea, tobacco, or sewage after a fall:
the river's not always cruel.

How long will those crumbs hang in the drift? Let them
carry to where the brine begins, then sink and settle,
add to the silt on stones he skimmed, fragments
of letter-freighting bottles, pins that fastened
matchwood rafts he saw propeller-churned to splinters.
From eighty years ago when the moon governed these games,
the river ran through his dreams.

He turned a bitter back as cranes swung over building sites
and the rattle of anchor chains gave way to shouted deals
from would-be Whittingtons. As houses grew where cows once grazed
so that Kennet, Colne and Wey were forced downstream,
and winter water spilled and spread back across ancient plains,
he shook his head: *Will they never learn?*
The river always wins.

GILL LEARNER · *Commended Prize*

Westwards to Bladon · WILFRED MORDEN

Homage

The complex traffic of this river's flow
forms patterns on the waves: bright pleasure boats
set off for Greenwich as a seagull floats.
I watch the up-and-down, the to-and-fro,
the skimming, chugging, churning, fast and slow;
small craft beneath the bridge, the blurred, remote
outline of larger ships and wharves. My throat
catches. That day, so many years ago,
saw one lone barge, black-draped, carry its load
in silence for a battle fought and won
as we recalled his words, the way he led.
Even the sceptics knew how much they owed.
And then the final tribute: one by one
tall cranes in Dockland bowed their metal heads.

BARBARA DANIELS · *First Prize*

Tower Bridge, sun and mist · TERENCE GILBERT

Community

A family of barges huddling together
in the shadow of Tower Bridge.
The elderly boats,
their age defined by rust
and sun-bleached colour,
carry the burden of their cargo
without a grumble.
The countless children,
bobbing excitedly to get attention,
are small tugs roped to their parents
so they won't wander off.
The wild character of the clan?
A houseboat clothed in blue paint,
with grass hair and a front-door mouth.
At certain times of day
you can enjoy their garden,
and see the bottles, trolleys and other litter,
sown by thoughtless visitors,
which bloom in the sand at low tide.

CLAUDIA BERKLEY

EIGHT
Ebb and flow

Eel-fare

April 1909 – you could stand
by the Thames holding a wooden sieve
or a bucket and they'd swim straight in,
a shimmy of rainbows running faster
than the tide. If you dipped a hand
they'd slipper over your skin like snakes,
seaweed-cold, diaphanous, a quick-
silver stream of liquid glass catching
the sun like the twist in a marble.

Eels, live eels, large river eels! seething
baskets of them, ninepence a pound.
*Spoon 'em up big, gov'nor, I could eat
a whale this arternoon!* By daylight
you'd sniggle them out of their holes
with a lob-worm on a stout needle
or plunge an eel-spear into the mud
where they slept. If you couldn't find bait,
you'd tear the lace-caps from an elder.

Sometimes they slithered out of the pot,
scarpered *ventre à terre* into the weeds
along the bank, as if they could smell
parsley and vinegar bubbling
in the stewpan. Often by the bridge
you'd see a heron with one corkscrewed
round its beak, flicking it, flipping it
high in the air until it slipped down
smooth and easy as a yard of ale.

Such a delicacy, a ha'p'orth
of hot eels straight from the coster's barrow,
or a *pâté aux anguilles* for less
than half-a-crown! Stir the century's
sludge for a flickering hologram
of those serpentine ghosts and wish them
safe passage past the river's anglers
back to their spawning grounds in the blue
waters of the warm Sargasso Sea.

SIRIOL TROUP · *Second Prize*

Eels · ROGER BARNES

Butlers Wharf · JULIET AYKROYD

page 48

Butlers Wharf

Comrats urges I loftiest hardnose to reconnoit it
so out I tails slinklike by light of drains
adown seweries glut with nongestibles
crushes through these stinkhigh tubulars and gushers
yo lowshoulders it by rank bums of cookeries
greasers − rubrimmers − sourgrates!
who'd as soon gets stamping I to gumbob − Ut! Ut!-
as tosses I scummings from their glistering bisons.

Now I cares nat a whiskered fillip for yells nor booters
but skimpers it bypast − mine ear cockadoo for crumbfall
stewscraps − spewbits − grublicks!
aught of goodgobble to fillup agog hungerpot
poor youngnips faintfort − comrats trewthly hopefort
on on roams I to this padfoot fishpong of a snackerplace
owhere finefur catch her pinkshell claws
in a plinkplunk to scrinch out windwhinings.

But I nat easy now to sound fret of strumbugs
but nowso deepdown loather of stareface fatsoles
whoso never glazes on I no nat mine sad starvelings
neither leaves us but shovelling up their carpet spatcrumbs
O gawk gawk I hates thlottery of unluckness
nay theasy blanketout of filthy richbins whoso snackup
spatch birds − blobster − syllablubbings
nay snubup hootings down mine black river of distreats.

Moan I : *wo care − wo kindiness − wo compassiabilities!*
I drabfull so and mouthless skeeters back to dumb comrats
mine hunghead bare and raw about the trewth and clause.

JULIET AYKROYD · *Commended Prize*

Detritus

Where the estuary meets the sea
global debris, tide-swept, piles high,
branch upon branch, criss-crossed.

Plastic bottles, transparent ones,
green coca cola, red and mauve ones,
a blue bucket chipped, one whole orange,

a bamboo stick, a rootless tree trunk
denuded, squashed aluminium cans,
dented milk cartons, tickets, plastic wrappers,

yellow twine, polystyrene globules gleaming white,
a terra cotta motorcycle helmet, five odd shoes,
one new, a pushchair spindle.

A sharp wind
No smell of chips
No smell of coffee behind plate glass
No seaside smell
No skateboards
No ice-cream vendors.

Obese herring gulls drift on the tide
turning and dipping for fish. They now
wheel inland again.

The sun smells cold. A tractor bulldozes
the flotsam and jetsam, scooping
the haemorrhaging of the seas.

It squeezes and squelches, scrunches and dips,
heaves and tips, until no footprint
remains, only sand.

EILEEN SPENCER TROTT

The poets, their poems and the illustrations

BARBARA ABBOTT lives on the banks of the Thames in Wraysbury. She started writing verse four years or so ago, and found it helped her through difficult times. Barbara loves not only the river but also the village of Wraysbury. It was the floods of January 2003 that inspired her to write *Jubilee River* – to record the feelings of the many villagers who had their homes flooded. (Note: Arthur Walters, the parish archivist, has given Barbara his permission for his words to be quoted.) A photograph by Sue Milton, a Thames Valley photographer, illustrates the poem.

ANNA ADAMS lives in Chiswick. She trained as an artist, but has concentrated on writing since the 1960s. Her poetry and prose are widely published, including her poem in the anthology which she compiled, *Thames – An anthology of river poems*, one of the inspirations for the RTS poetry competition. Anna's '**commended**' prize-winning poem, *View of Waterloo Bridge, from Hungerford Bridge*, captures the variety of moods of the view. The illustration chosen for this poem is by Roy Hammond, one of the Wapping Group of Artists. Anna's second poem selected for this anthology, *Two Cormorants*, is illustrated by her own watercolour.

BARRIE ARMSTRONG lives on Eel Pie Island, at Twickenham. He started his teaching career at Kingston Polytechnic, and is now semi-retired, helping out in Student Support at Richmond-upon-Thames College and at a centre for the homeless. Since childhood, Barrie has been fascinated with the River Thames. His poems have been published in a number of magazines. *River Praise*, which observes the behaviour of five different river birds, is a celebration of the wonderful spiritual life which they evoke. The kingfisher is depicted here by Roger Barnes.

JULIET AYKROYD has lived by Tower Bridge in Bermondsey for 26 years. She is an actress and playwright, and has had a number of poems published over the years. She is now busy growing gardens on moored barges on the Thames. Juliet says that she is well-acquainted with the local 'comrat population'. In her '**commended**' prize-winning poem, *Butlers Wharf*, she has let her imagination run, and has obviously had great fun inventing a 'rat' language. Juliet has also illustrated her poem with her watercolour, 'Butlers Wharf'.

ELIZABETH BELL lives on the river's edge in Lower Shiplake. She has been a painter and printmaker for many years, and started writing more recently, in the late 1990s. Elizabeth has found that each of the two disciplines contributes to the other. She uses the River Thames and its wildlife as inspiration for both painting and writing. Two of her poems have been selected for this anthology, *Memory of Migration* and *Light*. Elizabeth has illustrated the latter with her own watercolour.

CLAUDIA BERKLEY moved close to the Thames in Southwark in 1999, and walking by the river on Sunday mornings quickly became part of her life. She feels it was inevitable that at some time she would try to capture aspects of these walks in poetry, and *Community*, is one such example. Claudia wishes that she could write full-time as she finds her poetry is a wonderful way of capturing the little details of life that may otherwise be forgotten or go unnoticed. Terence Gilbert's painting, 'Tower Bridge, sun and mist', has been chosen to illustrate this poem.

ROBERT DE BOARD has lived in Henley since the 1970s, and has attended every Henley Regatta during that time, and on a variety of boats, especially his own narrowboat. In his poem, *Going to the Regatta*, he wanted to poke gentle fun at the middle classes at play, including himself! He chose the style of John Betjeman, as a homage to one of his favourite poets. Robert has also been inspired to poetry by the imaginative world of Toad and Ratty, created by the Cookham writer, Kenneth Grahame, in *The Wind in the Willows*. His poem here is illustrated with a painting by Terence Gilbert.

BERNARD BOYS is a Chartered Structural Engineer who retired in 2000. He has written a few poems over the last twenty years and, being a life-long cyclist, most of these have appeared in his cycling club's magazine. Bernard was born and raised in Battersea, close to the park and the river. He has developed a close affinity with the Thames, moving house to Staines riverside in 1987. He wrote his poem *Riverside Living* in early spring of that year. He has been an active member of the River Thames Society for many years.

JULIAN COLTON lives in Selkirk, in Scotland, where he is a widely-published poet, including having a poetry pamphlet, *Something for the Weekend*, published by the Scottish Borders Council Arts Service. He is currently co-editor of the literary magazine, *The Eildon Tree*, published from the Scottish Borders. Julian wrote his poem, *Thames River Odyssey*, after a short visit to London. While crossing the river on a train by Waterloo, the idea came to him of a poem reflecting all the river's history.

GORDON COPE is a Canadian writer who was based in Henley-on-Thames, and who has now returned to Canada. For a year or more, he had the pleasure of observing the Thames in its many seasons and moods. Gordon notes that the ever-changing river inspired his poem, *Dusk*, and has been a major inspiration as he worked on his latest travel memoir, *The Henley Diaries*.

LES CROWHURST lives on the edge of the Gade Valley in Hertfordshire. He was born in Oxfordshire and feels a strong affinity with the Thames, having boated on it, fished it, walked it, and even fallen in it! He is currently helping with the Wildlife Trust's Otter Survey on the Loddon tributary. Les has written a number of poems and stories about the river, and wrote *The River God* inspired by the floods of 2003, and the sheer power of the river pushing through at Cookham Bridge. A photograph by Susan Martin illustrates the poem.

BARBARA DANIELS is now living in Monmouthshire in Wales. She started writing poetry late in life, but has won prizes in many competitions, and had five booklets of poems published. Her sonnet, *Homage*, was awarded **first prize** in the RTS competition, for which it was specially written. Barbara was intent on capturing the busy but peaceful atmosphere of the river now, and contrasting it with the day of Sir Winston Churchill's funeral and the moment when the cranes were dipped in salute for him. The poem is a tribute both to him and to the river.

The poem is illustrated, with the kind permission of the Museum in Docklands, by Wilfred Morden's painting, 'Westwards to Bladon'. This was commissioned by the Port of London Authority, to commemorate the occasion of the state funeral, on 30 January 1965. The painting shows the *Havengore*, the PLA launch, bearing the coffin of Sir Winston on its Thames journey upstream from Tower Pier to Festival Pier.

JILL FINDLAY lives by the Thames at Wargrave, and is very conscious of the river in all its moods, particularly when the level rises. The floods in January 2003 were the worst she had experienced in 28 years, with the water four feet deep across her garden and up the lane almost to Wargrave Station. In the end, Jill and her husband had to be rescued by four firemen in their inflatable dinghy. So the image of the Thames in flood was very fresh in her mind when she wrote her poem, *On going to see the Thames in flood*.

ANNE JENKINS is a chartered accountant and writer, living on the banks of the Thames in Staines in Middlesex. She writes mainly short stories. Her poem, *River Thames, January 2003*, was her first attempt at poetry and was inspired by the rapidly advancing waters of the 2003 flooding. Since then, Anne has had another poem short-listed in an annual Arts Council sponsored competition.

LAURA KAYNE is currently living in Brighton, East Sussex, and undertaking an MA in Creative and Critical Writing at the University of Sussex. She worked for two years at a London publishing company before deciding to return to studying and to concentrate on developing her creative writing. Laura has been writing short stories and occasional poetry since her teenage years. *Watching the River* is the first of her poems to be published. The artist, Suzanne-Lizette Strand, a graduate of the Royal Academy Schools, has illustrated this poem.

DR DOREEN KING lives in Hornchurch, east of London. She is a Fellow of the Wellcome Trust, and researcher in Medicine and the Arts, at King's College, London. She is a poetry critic for New Hope International. Doreen is best known as a haiku poet, and had an exhibition of her haiga at the London Barbican in 2003. Her poem, *I want to see a daffodil on Big Ben* is a light-hearted piece, illustrated here by Annie Stevens. The poem was written for a poet and friend, Sara Boyes. (Editor's note: Sara Boyes' poem, *Wild Flowers*, appears in the anthology of the same name which she edited in 1993.)

WENDY KLEIN is a dual national, UK/US, who has lived near the Thames since 1971. She has a Diploma in Creative Writing from the Continuing Education Department of Oxford University. Her first novel, *Listening for Nightingales*, was published in 2002, and she has since worked on a collection of poems. Wendy contributes to poetry readings, has published poems in *The Jewish Quarterly* and has been successful in the Ver Poets Competition. She enjoys walking her cocker spaniels by the Thames in Pangbourne, where her poem, *Autumn*, is set.

GRAHAM KNIGHT lives in Carshalton, Surrey, and has been writing poetry in his leisure moments for many years. A frequent visitor to the river, he has walked the Thames Path from the Barrier to the source. He continues to be fascinated by the variety of activities on and around the river and the intriguing history behind the unusual names he discovers on his travels such as that of Halfpenny Bridge at Lechlade. Graham wrote his poem, *Halfpenny Bridge*, in 1999. It is illustrated here by the artist, Roger Barnes.

GILL LEARNER lives in Reading. She has always loved language, but not until she retired in 1999 did she have the time to devote to writing. She has been drawn to poetry in more recent years. She reads contemporary poems of all kinds and attends poetry-writing classes. Her inspiration comes from everywhere. Gill says that quite often a character and sometimes a narrative emerge in a most unexpected way, as in her '**commended**' prize-winning poem, *Belonging*, written early in 2003.

ALWYN MARRIAGE, now living in Guildford, Surrey, has been a university philosophy lecturer, a director of two international aid agencies and the editor of a journal. She is the author of four books and numerous articles and poems, and is at present working as an Environmental Consultant. Alwyn has written poetry all her life. *Charting the Thames* was written specially for the RTS competition, which she entered because she loves the River Thames.

LORNA PATTERSON lives by the River Pang in the Berkshire Downs. She has taught English for many years, but only started to write poetry about three years ago. Lorna knows the Thames best along the stretch between Oxford and Reading, which she has explored on foot and in a dinghy with her children. The original idea for her poem, *Painting at Kew*, came from looking at old photographs.

GEOFF PAYNE has lived by the Thames in several periods of his life, and currently lives in Staines, Middlesex. He is an active member of the River Thames Society. Geoff had a basically technical education and career, in which clarity and precision in language was important. He enjoys writing a variety of styles of poetry. His poem, *The Thames Rivers*, which was written for the RTS competition, provides a record, in sequence, of all the Rivers that are confluent tributaries of the Thames.

ENID PHILIP has a third-floor flat close to the river in Caversham, near Reading. Its large windows mirror the river in its many moods. Her poem, *The River Thames apologises*, was written during the floods of January 2003, as a contribution to a poetry workshop in Reading. It was through this workshop that Enid heard of the River Thames Society's competition. A photograph by Sue Milton, a Thames Valley photographer, illustrates the poem.

ANGELA RIGBY lives in Ealing in West London. Her childhood home was a mill on the Colne, a peaceful tributary that joins the Thames at Staines. She particularly loves the Thames at Hungerford Bridge, which is described in her poem, *Crossing to the South Bank*. Angela is widely published and recently brought out a poetry collection, *The deep darkness of love*. She is an artist as well as a poet. Her poem has been illustrated by Suzanne-Lizette Strand, a graduate of the Royal Academy Schools.

DR JOSEPH RYAN lives next to the Thames, overlooking Ash Island and the weir by Molesey Lock. He works as a freelance writer, editor, researcher and photographer. He has written or edited over one hundred books and articles. Joseph's vision of the world is currently largely shaped by his photographic and Zen Buddhist practice. His poem, *Winter River (at Hampton Court)*, was partly written as a response to a series of photographs of the river taken by Susan Martin. Her long-exposure photograph of lights near Thames Ditton Island illustrates the poem.

DAPHNE SCHILLER lives in St Albans. She has been writing poetry since the 1960s, has won prizes in competitions and been published in magazines. Her last collection, *The Scarlet Fish*, came out in 2002. Daphne's poem '*What I like most of all about London is the fog*', was written specially for the competition. It was inspired by Monet's paintings of the Thames. It is illustrated here, with the kind permission of the Yamagata Museum of Art in Japan, by Monet's painting 'Charing Cross Bridge, the Thames', 1903.

GILL SMITH lives in Reading, and has been writing poetry of sorts since she was at school. She has had poetry published in a number of magazines. Gill writes both serious and comic verse, so her poem, *Liquid History*, includes a little of both. It was inspired by the fact that there's so much to say about the Thames — this seemed the best way of fitting it all into one poem.

EILEEN SPENCER TROTT has lived in Reading for thirty five years. The town embraces an extensive curve of the Thames which she explores on foot and by boat in all seasons. She has written intermittently for as long as she can remember, particularly poetry, stories for children and more recently her autobiography. Eileen's inspiration comes from all aspects of her life, but particularly from travelling. Many of her poems have been published. Her poem, *Detritus*, captures one of the many moods of the estuary river.

SIRIOL TROUP lives close to the river in Twickenham. She has been writing poetry for a year or two, has been successful in several competitions, and had a small collection published. Siriol had intended to write a poem about the nearby Eel Pie Island, a favourite haunt for her family. During her research she became fascinated by the eels themselves, the history of fishing for them in the Thames, and in the vocabulary associated with eel-fishing. Her poem, *Eel-fare*, was awarded **second prize** in the RTS competition. It is illustrated here by the artist, Roger Barnes.

JENYTH WORSLEY now lives in Oxford. She has always loved rivers, having spent her childhood near the Zambezi. Jenyth has written poetry for some years, and has been a semi-finalist in the national Speak-a-Poem Competition. As a producer in BBC Radio, it was part of her job to encourage others in writing and speaking, and she now enjoys having the opportunity to do both. Her 'commended' prize-winning poem, *Tamasá Reaches*, is inspired by her many visits and walks by the Thames, particularly in Barnes and along the Upper Thames. The poem has been illustrated by Dianne Cockburn, an artist who also lives in Oxford.

PETER WYTON lives in Gloucester. Having retired from three decades in the Royal Air Force, he is now employed in the communication centre of a national security company. He has five volumes of poetry to his credit and has performed his work at numerous venues country-wide, including the Henley Arts Festival on the banks of the Thames. With his flying background, Peter is aware that RAF planes are a regular feature over the Upper Thames Valley. Hence the reference to a droning Hercules in his poem, *The Legless Ballet*. The poem has been illustrated by Dianne Cockburn.

The Poetry Competition

The River Thames Society's first national poetry competition was held over the winter of 2002–03. Entrants were invited to submit poems, with a maximum of 40 lines, inspired by, or related to, the River Thames. The competition was announced in the *Thames Guardian*, the RTS magazine, and was advertised widely by the Poetry Library based at the Royal Festival Hall, and in libraries and poetry workshops along the length of the Thames. Over 140 poems were received. These were judged initially by Jane Draycott and Virginia Winfield and the six winning entries were selected by the poet, Wendy Cope. These were announced in April 2003, and published on the RTS website.

The Editor

Val Mason has lived on the Bray Reach of the Thames since 1996. She has always loved being in or near water, taking part in a variety of watersports. She enjoys the restful pace of boating on the Thames. An occasional poet herself, Val organised the River Thames Society's first national poetry competition, and has edited this resultant anthology, selecting the poems and the illustrations. Her previous publications include a number of government social research reports. Val is one of the directors of the RTS, and is active on planning and flooding issues.

River Thames Society

The River Thames Society was founded in 1962 by a group of people concerned about the deterioration of the river environment. The Society soon became known as the 'Voice of the River', campaigning for the construction of the Thames Barrier, supporting boat clubs in danger of losing their premises, instigating the Thames Traditional Boat Rally and taking many other initiatives. Over the years, the Society has educated, persuaded and encouraged those who work, play or live on or near the river, to value it, to respect it and to enjoy it.

The Society is currently campaigning for strategic planning and increased funding for the river, and for sustainable regeneration on the Thames Tideway. Following its work on a strategy for the future planning and management of the river and its floodplain, the Society was instrumental in the setting up of the River Thames Alliance in 2003, bringing together all authorities and organisations with an interest in the River Thames.

The Society's members contribute to the life of the Thames in a wide variety of ways – acting as river wardens, promoting nature conservation, campaigning for boating and recreational facilities, taking part in traditional rowing in the Society's cutter, organising talks and social events related to the river, commenting on planning proposals and on flooding issues, and now encouraging poetry and art related to the river.

FOR FURTHER INFORMATION

Please visit our website: www.riverthamessociety.org.uk

or email: admin@riverthamessociety.org.uk

or write to: River Thames Society, Side House, Middle Assendon, Henley-on-Thames, Oxfordshire, RG9 6AP

Thames Heritage Trust

The Thames Heritage Trust was formed in 1979 by the late John Coleman OBE. The Trust aims to preserve and enhance the rich heritage of the Thames. It provides grants and loans for volunteer-led projects that develop or improve leisure, cultural or education facilities alongside the non-tidal Thames.

Working in conjunction with other River Thames organisations, such as the River Thames Society, the Trust uses funds raised from individual donations and legacies to help and encourage different initiatives involving the Thames.

FOR FURTHER INFORMATION

Please write to: Thames Heritage Trust, Millbrook, The Warren, East Horsley, Surrey, KT24 5RH